"SUSTAINABLE DEVELOPMENT, DEMOCRACY AND PEACE ARE INDIVISIBLE."

— Wangari Maathai

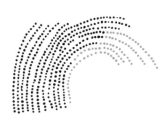

CONTENTS

SPEECH
Wangari Maathai's Nobel Peace Prize Acceptance Speech

9

KEYS TO THE SPEECH
The First African Woman to Receive the Nobel Peace Price

59

"I accept it on behalf of the people of Kenya and Africa, and indeed the world."   62

"My inspiration partly comes from my childhood experiences and observations of Nature."   65

"The challenge is to restore the home of the tadpoles and give back to our children a world of beauty and wonder."   67

"Tree planting became a natural choice."   68

"Our people have been persuaded to believe that because they are poor, they lack ... knowledge and skills to address their challenges."   71

"Responsible governance of the environment was impossible without democratic space."   73

"We are called to assist the Earth to heal her wounds and in the process heal our own."   77

Wangari Maathai's Nobel Peace Prize Acceptance Speech

Oslo, December 10, 2004

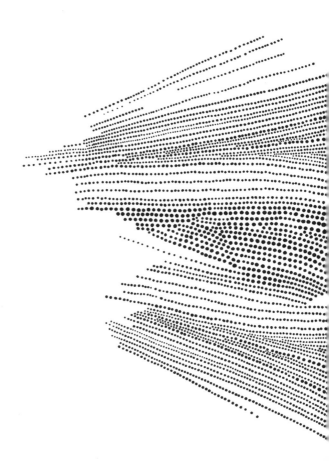

Your Majesties,

Your Royal Highnesses, Honorable Members of the Norwegian Nobel Committee, Excellencies, Ladies and Gentlemen,

I stand before you and the world humbled by this recognition and uplifted by the honor of being the 2004 Nobel Peace Laureate.

As the first African woman to receive this prize, I accept it on behalf of the people of Kenya and Africa, and indeed the world. I am especially mindful of women and the girl child. I hope it will encourage them to raise their voices and take more space for leadership. I know the honor also gives a deep sense of pride to our men, both old and young. As a mother, I appreciate the inspiration this brings to the youth and urge them to use it to pursue their dreams.

"I hope it will encourage them to raise their voices."

Although this prize comes to me, it acknowledges the work of countless individuals and groups across the globe. They work quietly and often without recognition to protect the environment, promote democracy, defend human rights and ensure equality between women and men. By so doing, they plant seeds of peace. I know they, too, are proud today. To all who feel represented by this prize I say use it to advance your mission and meet the high expectations the world will place on us.

"This prize ... acknowledges the work of countless individuals and groups across the globe."

This honor is also for my family, friends, partners and supporters throughout the world. All of them helped shape the vision and sustain our work, which was often accomplished under hostile conditions. I am also grateful to the people of Kenya — who remained stubbornly hopeful that democracy could be realized and their environment managed sustainably. Because of this support, I am here today to accept this great honor.

I am immensely privileged to join my fellow African Peace laureates, Presidents Nelson Mandela and F.W. de Klerk, Archbishop Desmond Tutu, the late Chief Albert Luthuli, the late Anwar el-Sadat and the UN Secretary General, Kofi Annan.

"I am also grateful to the people of Kenya."

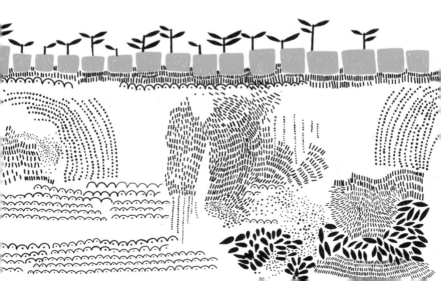

"Let us embrace democratic governance, protect human rights and protect our environment."

I know that African people everywhere are encouraged by this news. My fellow Africans, as we embrace this recognition, let us use it to intensify our commitment to our people, to reduce conflicts and poverty and thereby improve their quality of life. Let us embrace democratic governance, protect human rights and protect our environment. I am confident that we shall rise to the occasion. I have always believed that solutions to most of our problems must come from us.

In this year's prize, the Norwegian Nobel Committee has placed the critical issue of environment and its linkage to democracy and peace before the world. For their visionary action, I am profoundly grateful. Recognizing that sustainable development, democracy and peace are indivisible is an idea whose time has come. Our work over the past thirty years has always appreciated and engaged these linkages.

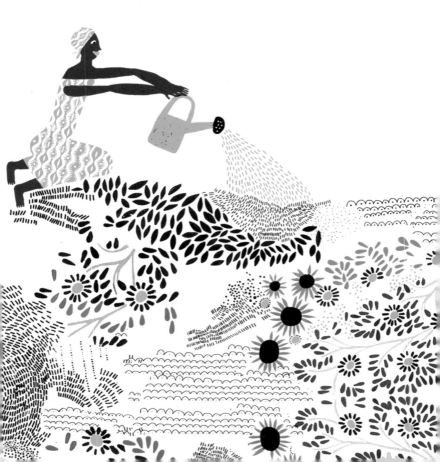

"Sustainable development, democracy and peace are indivisible."

My inspiration partly comes from my childhood experiences and observations of Nature in rural Kenya. It has been influenced and nurtured by the formal education I was privileged to receive in Kenya, the United States and Germany. As I was growing up, I witnessed forests being cleared and replaced by commercial plantations, which destroyed local biodiversity and the capacity of the forests to conserve water.

"As I was growing up,
I witnessed forests being
cleared and replaced by
commercial plantations."

"Throughout Africa, women are the primary caretakers."

Excellencies, ladies and gentlemen,

In 1977, when we started the Green Belt Movement, I was partly responding to needs identified by rural women, namely lack of firewood, clean drinking water, balanced diets, shelter and income.

Throughout Africa, women are the primary caretakers, holding significant responsibility for tilling the land and feeding their families. As a result, they are often the first to become aware of environmental damage as resources become scarce and incapable of sustaining their families.

"When the environment is destroyed ... we undermine our quality of life and that of future generations."

The women we worked with recounted that, unlike in the past, they were unable to meet their basic needs. This was due to the degradation of their immediate environment as well as the introduction of commercial farming, which replaced the growing of household food crops. But international trade controlled the price of the exports from these small-scale farmers, and a reasonable and just income could not be guaranteed. I came to understand that when the environment is destroyed, plundered or mismanaged, we undermine our quality of life and that of future generations.

Tree planting became a natural choice to address some of the initial basic needs identified by women. Also, tree planting is simple, attainable and guarantees quick, successful results within a reasonable amount of time. This sustains interest and commitment.

So, together, we have planted over thirty million trees that provide fuel, food, shelter and income to support their children's education and household needs. The activity also creates employment and improves soils and watersheds. Through their involvement, women gain some degree of power over their lives, especially their social and economic position and relevance in the family. This work continues.

"Together, we have planted over thirty million trees that provide fuel, food, shelter and income."

"Historically our people have been persuaded to believe ... that solutions to their problems must come from 'outside.'"

Initially, the work was difficult because historically our people have been persuaded to believe that because they are poor, they lack not only capital, but also knowledge and skills to address their challenges. Instead they are conditioned to believe that solutions to their problems must come from "outside." Further, women did not realize that meeting their needs depended on their environment being healthy and well managed. They were also unaware that a degraded environment leads to a scramble for scarce resources and may culminate in poverty and even conflict. They were also unaware of the injustices of international economic arrangements.

In order to assist communities to understand these linkages, we developed a citizen-education program, during which people identify their problems, the causes and possible solutions. They then make connections between their own personal actions and the problems they witness in the environment and in society. They learn that our world is confronted with a litany of woes: corruption, violence against women and children, disruption and breakdown of families, and disintegration of cultures and communities. They also identify the abuse of drugs and chemical substances, especially among young people. There are also devastating diseases that are defying cures or occurring in epidemic proportions. Of particular concern are HIV/AIDS, malaria and diseases associated with malnutrition.

"Our world is confronted with a litany of woes."

On the environment front, they are exposed to many human activities that are devastating to the environment and societies. These include widespread destruction of ecosystems, especially through deforestation, climatic instability and contamination in the soils and waters that all contribute to excruciating poverty.

In the process, the participants discover that they must be part of the solutions. They realize their hidden potential and are empowered to overcome inertia and take action. They come to recognize that they are the primary custodians and beneficiaries of the environment that sustains them.

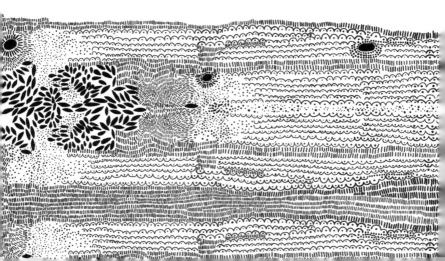

"The participants discover that they must be part of the solutions."

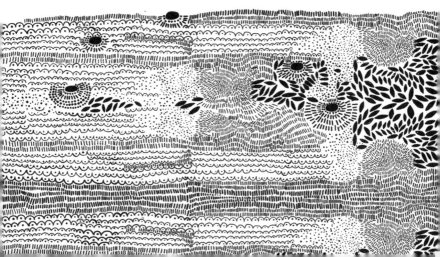

Entire communities also come to understand that while it is necessary to hold their governments accountable, it is equally important that in their own relationships with each other, they exemplify the leadership values they wish to see in their own leaders, namely justice, integrity and trust.

Although initially the Green Belt Movement's tree-planting activities did not address issues of democracy and peace, it soon became clear that responsible governance of the environment was impossible without democratic space. Therefore, the tree became a symbol for the democratic struggle in Kenya. Citizens were mobilized to challenge widespread abuses of power, corruption and environmental mismanagement. In Nairobi's Uhuru Park, at Freedom Corner, and in many parts of the country, trees of peace were planted to demand the release of prisoners of conscience and a peaceful transition to democracy.

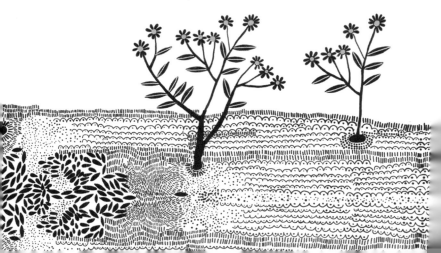

"The tree became a symbol for the democratic struggle in Kenya."

"Through the Green Belt Movement, thousands of ordinary citizens were mobilized and empowered to take action and effect change."

Through the Green Belt Movement, thousands of ordinary citizens were mobilized and empowered to take action and effect change. They learned to overcome fear and a sense of helplessness and moved to defend democratic rights.

In time, the tree also became a symbol for peace and conflict resolution, especially during ethnic conflicts in Kenya when the Green Belt Movement used peace trees to reconcile disputing communities. During the ongoing rewriting of the Kenyan constitution, similar trees of peace were planted in many parts of the country to promote a culture of peace. Using trees as a symbol of peace is in keeping with a widespread African tradition. For example, the elders of the Kikuyu carried a staff from the thigi tree that, when placed between two disputing sides, caused them to stop fighting and seek reconciliation. Many communities in Africa have these traditions.

Such practices are part of an extensive cultural heritage, which contributes both to the conservation of habitats and to cultures of peace. With the destruction of these cultures and the introduction of new values, local biodiversity is no longer valued or protected and as a result, it is quickly degraded and disappears. For this reason, the Green Belt Movement explores the concept of cultural biodiversity, especially with respect to indigenous seeds and medicinal plants.

"Such practices are part of an extensive cultural heritage."

As we progressively understood the causes of environmental degradation, we saw the need for good governance. Indeed, the state of any county's environment is a reflection of the kind of governance in place, and without good governance there can be no peace. Many countries, which have poor governance systems, are also likely to have conflicts and poor laws protecting the environment.

In 2002, the courage, resilience, patience and commitment of members of the Green Belt Movement, other civil society organizations and the Kenyan public culminated in the peaceful transition to a democratic government and laid the foundation for a more stable society.

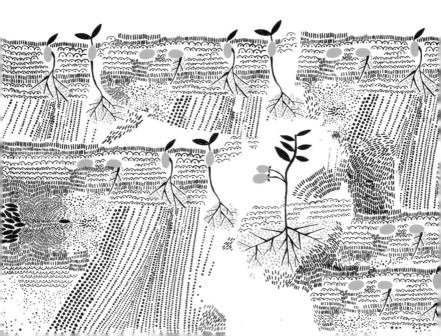

"The state of any country's environment is a reflection of the kind of governance in place."

Excellencies, friends, ladies and gentlemen,

It is thirty years since we started this work. Activities that devastate the environment and societies continue unabated. Today we are faced with a challenge that calls for a shift in our thinking, so that humanity stops threatening its life-support system. We are called to assist the Earth to heal her wounds and in the process heal our own — indeed, to embrace the whole creation in all its diversity, beauty and wonder. This will happen if we see the need to revive our sense of belonging to a larger family of life, with which we have shared our evolutionary process.

"Activities
that devastate
the environment
and societies
continue unabated."

In the course of history, there comes a time when humanity is called to shift to a new level of consciousness, to reach a higher moral ground. A time when we have to shed our fear and give hope to each other.

That time is now.

The Norwegian Nobel Committee has challenged the world to broaden the understanding of peace: there can be no peace without equitable development; and there can be no development without sustainable management of the environment in a democratic and peaceful space. This shift is an idea whose time has come.

"There comes a time ... when we have to shed our fear and give hope to each other."

I call on leaders, especially from Africa, to expand democratic space and build fair and just societies that allow the creativity and energy of their citizens to flourish. Those of us who have been privileged to receive education, skills and experiences and even power must be role models for the next generation of leadership. In this regard, I would also like to appeal for the freedom of my fellow laureate Aung San Suu Kyi so that she can continue her work for peace and democracy for the people of Burma* and the world at large.

*Myanmar

"I call on leaders,
especially from Africa,
to expand
democratic space."

"Culture plays a central role in the political, economic and social life of communities."

Culture plays a central role in the political, economic and social life of communities. Indeed, culture may be the missing link in the development of Africa. Culture is dynamic and evolves over time, consciously discarding retrogressive traditions, like female genital mutilation (FGM), and embracing aspects that are good and useful.

Africans, especially, should rediscover positive aspects of their culture. In accepting them, they would give themselves a sense of belonging, identity and self-confidence.

Ladies and gentlemen,

There is also need to galvanize civil society and grassroots movements to catalyze change. I call upon governments to recognize the role of these social movements in building a critical mass of responsible citizens, who help maintain checks and balances in society. On their part, civil society should embrace not only their rights but also their responsibilities.

Further, industry and global institutions must appreciate that ensuring economic justice, equity and ecological integrity are of greater value than profits at any cost. The extreme global inequities and prevailing consumption patterns continue at the expense of the environment and peaceful co-existence. The choice is ours.

"I call upon governments to recognize the role of these social movements."

"You are our hope and our future."

I would like to call on young people to commit themselves to activities that contribute toward achieving their long-term dreams. They have the energy and creativity to shape a sustainable future. To the young people I say, you are a gift to your communities and indeed the world. You are our hope and our future.

The holistic approach to development, as exemplified by the Green Belt Movement, could be embraced and replicated in more parts of Africa and beyond. It is for this reason that I have established the Wangari Maathai Foundation to ensure the continuation and expansion of these activities. Although a lot has been achieved, much remains to be done.

Excellencies, ladies and gentlemen,

As I conclude, I reflect on my childhood experience when I would visit a stream next to our home to fetch water for my mother. I would drink water straight from the stream. Playing among the arrowroot leaves, I tried in vain to pick up the strands of frogs' eggs, believing they were beads. But every time I put my little fingers under them they would break. Later, I saw thousands of tadpoles: black, energetic and wriggling through the clear water against the background of the brown earth. This is the world I inherited from my parents.

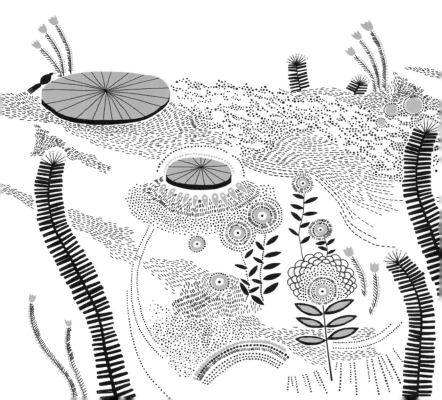

"This is the world
I inherited
from my parents."

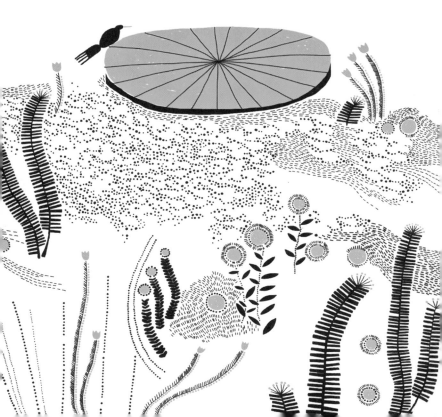

Today, over fifty years later, the stream has dried up, women walk long distances for water, which is not always clean, and children will never know what they have lost. The challenge is to restore the home of the tadpoles and give back to our children a world of beauty and wonder.

Thank you very much.

KEYS TO THE SPEECH
The First African Woman to Receive the Nobel Peace Prize

Commentary by Laia de Ahumada
Translated by Susan Ouriou

On December 10, 2004, in the city of Oslo, Norway, Wangari Maathai gave her speech accepting the Nobel Peace Prize.

The prize, awarded to people or institutions having worked to promote peace, was founded by Alfred B. Nobel (1833-1896) who, paradoxically, had dedicated his life to inventing and manufacturing arms and explosives, including dynamite, with which he amassed a great fortune. In 1888, in a French newspaper, Alfred Nobel read an obituary titled "The merchant of death is dead." Actually, the person who had died was his brother Ludvig, a petroleum entrepreneur, but the reporter had confused the two and thought it was Alfred, the arms manufacturer, who had died. Alfred was so upset by the article that he began to reflect on his life and eventually dedicated nearly his entire fortune to instituting the awards that bore his name.

Those awards are granted to people who have distinguished themselves in one of five areas: Physics, Chemistry, Physiology or Medicine, Literature and Peace. And so, the Nobel Peace Prize is meant to award efforts to promote peace, which Nobel's weapons had made even more fragile. The same weapons with which Wangari was confronted as she worked on behalf of the environment, democracy and human rights in her country of birth, Kenya.

Wangari Maathai was the first African woman to be awarded the Nobel Peace Prize. It was also the first time that the prize included defense of the environment as a key element to ensuring peace. Wangari was also the first woman from East Africa to receive a PhD in biology, to head up a university department and to obtain a university chair.

However, most important of all is that she was a woman who knew how to use what she'd learned and what she firmly believed to help her people and the world. Wangari Maathai was a leader (possibly influenced by the charisma of the Anjirû clan, one of the ten clans in the Kikuyu community to which she belonged). She was a leader because she prioritized others' interests over her own and used her talents in the service of others, working with them to achieve the common good, convinced that every person's future lies in their own hands.

"I accept it on behalf of the people of Kenya and Africa, and indeed the world."

For the awarding of the Nobel prize, Wangari Maathai gets to her feet and makes her way to the podium with what might seem like timid steps, although they have nothing to do with self-consciousness and everything to do with the care of someone who knows the connection of walking barefoot on the earth. She wears a copper-colored dress and headwrap, having chosen a warm color that inspires energy and dynamism. Once at the microphone, her first move is to smile with a look in her eye that gives a glimpse of both her inner tenderness and strength. She pulls out the speech from her folder and her smile gives way to a more serious expression (one she no doubt has had to adopt when confronting police, oligarchs and politicians) as, her voice tinged with emotion, she begins to speak. Her eyes light up and her attitude becomes more intense.

Her first act is to accept the prize on behalf of her country Kenya, the African continent and the entire world, convinced that this recognition of an African woman will encourage all women to take up leadership spaces. Next come her thanks, during which she highlights the three themes she will develop during her lecture, the three fronts on which she fights: the environment, human rights and democratic government.

It is a speech free of abstraction that underscores the responsibility that lies with people. She speaks of equal rights for women, but also of the importance of convincing women of their ability to defend those rights; she speaks of advocating for the environment, but also of the need for people to realize it is their job to defend it. The African continent, reeling from the effects of colonization, must take back its right to make decisions around its own resources in order to protect them as had been done since ancient times. She is aware that any fight on behalf of the Earth and all Earth's creatures is a fight for a life of dignity, justice and peace. She urges men and women to empower themselves and follow their dreams since she is convinced that they can make those dreams come true if only they set their minds to it. She believes that everyone is capable of being the change they want to see, explaining, "I have always believed that solutions to most of our problems must come from us."

The themes she develops throughout her speech are keystones in a life led in pursuit of one desire: to heal the Earth of its wounds, knowing that by doing so, each and every person living there will be healed as well. It is a desire that comes from deep within, from her own experience, and that continues outward, toward her community and the world.

She echoes that experience as she concludes her thanks and launches into the substance of her speech, first stating, "My inspiration partly comes from my childhood experiences and observations of Nature." The tale of one such childhood experience, about the stream and the frogs' eggs, serves as the conclusion to her lecture as well. This act of storytelling is a nod to the oral tradition of her country and to the important role that tales and legends have played in transmitting knowledge and values. Wangari demonstrates the need to reclaim the cultural traditions that are part of her country's identity.

At the beginning and end of her speech, Wangari explains where she comes from and what has influenced her, and reminisces about the world she inherited from her parents — a world teeming with life, which she is committed to restoring.

"My inspiration partly comes from my childhood experiences and observations of Nature."

Wangari was born on April 1, 1940, in rural Nyeri in central Kenya on fertile land with views of Mount Kenya, a mountain deemed to be sacred. Her mother Wanjiru Kibicho and her father Muta Njugi were farmers. They gave her her paternal grandmother's name, Wangari, and her father's name, Muta. Years later, when she married, she added her husband's last name and became Wangari Muta Maathai.

Wangari was the third of six children, and as a female and the eldest daughter in her family, she was, along with her mother, expected to take care of her siblings and the household tasks, fetching water and tending the garden. Her memories are those of a family-centered and tribal community, of natural abundance and respect for people and for nature. Her father was polygamous, a custom among the Kikuyu, and could marry as many women as he wished, with the obligation to support them and his children. Her mother was one of her father's four wives, and Wangari has fond memories of belonging to a large family in which she never felt alone. Of her mother, she remembers that she never spoke a harsh word to her daughter, only words of wisdom. Of her father, she remembers the importance he placed on the education of all his children. Which is why she was able to go to school at a time when education was a privilege (and if you were female, even more so, since you were expected to help around the house and to marry young). At the age of seven, she started elementary school at a Catholic mission a forty-five minute walk from her house. Afterward, she was able to pursue her secondary studies in a Catholic boarding school run by the Sisters of Loreto in Limuru, not far from Nairobi. In 1960, she won a Kennedy scholarship, which was awarded by the United States for the promotion of education for young Africans. It was unusual to see an African girl travel to a faraway country chiefly inhabited by White people. Many neighbors didn't understand; they felt she was betraying her tradition and they clashed with her mother, but Wanjiru defended her daughter. For Wangari as well, the experience was a cultural shock somewhat lessened by the fact that she found herself in a college run by nuns in an environment similar to the school she'd attended in Kenya. She said that she learned passion and tenacity from the nuns, as well as solidarity and caring for others — qualities that helped her as a leader.

In the United States, she graduated with a Masters' degree in biology but also learned about the fundamental principles of democracy and feminism, which allowed her to see herself differently — as a respected citizen, responsible and free. She loved studying, but her greatest desire was to return as soon as possible to her own country and implement what she had learned. And she did: she returned to Kenya and, not without difficulty, landed a position as a professor at the University of Nairobi. In 1967, she married Mwangi Mathai (adding an *a* to her husband's surname to have it read the way it sounded, *Maathai*), a sociologist, economist and politician, and soon after left for two years in Germany where she earned her PhD in veterinary biology.

Wangari specialized in research into the life cycles of a parasite that attacked livestock. She felt her research would help fight disease and mortality in cattle. This led her to travel through Kenya's rural areas in search of samples. It was then that she saw the changes her country had undergone during her few years abroad: primarily, the massive clearing of forests in order to plant export crops such as coffee or tea and the ensuing erosion and loss of soil nutrients and the pollution of rivers with sediment.

"The challenge is to restore the home of the tadpoles and give back to our children a world of beauty and wonder."

This is the last sentence in Wangari Muta Maathai's speech. This is the challenge she issues to the whole world. It is born of a profound experience dating back to her childhood that, later, with her academic training and expertise, she was able to express to the wider community. An experience inspired by the nature she so revered and loved.

Not far from her home was a fig tree from which a stream sprang. The fig tree was considered sacred by the Kikuyu because water was always to be found nearby. Her mother used to tell her that she must not take wood from that tree and that she must look after it, saying often that a tree is

of wood for today's fire but of growing trees for tomorrow; it generates employment since it allows women to earn money for every planted tree that survives; it promotes gender equality since women who earn an income are better regarded; and, in environmental terms, tree planting does not just give access to firewood, but also to the regeneration of the soil and a return to biodiversity.

Thus, in 1977, the Green Belt Movement was born, and since then it has planted over fifty million trees in Kenya with a view to improving the environment and people's lives. And with it, Wangari Maathai, the originator of the movement who was already the mother of three children at the time, also became Mama Miti, "the mother of the trees."

The first thing the women did was to learn how to plant trees. Initially, the seeds were provided by nurseries, but soon there were so many women involved in tree planting that there weren't enough nurseries to supply them. The women were then taught how to band together and create nurseries of their own. That way, they depended on no one. They were independent. They taught one another, and the nurseries multiplied. If they planted a tree and it survived, the Movement compensated them with a small sum that allowed them to improve their situation within their communities, motivating them even further.

It was obvious that poor environmental management led to problems for people. Wangari clearly saw that, besides planting trees, consciousness-raising work needed to be done with the women who complained of the symptoms yet needed to understand the root causes and fight to alleviate them. The women had to recognize the need to both protect the environment and defend their own rights: they needed to plant trees and sow ideas. Therefore, the Movement gave training not just in gardening but also in feminism, politics and ecology. As Wangari explains in her speech, "In the process, the participants discover that they must be part of the solutions." They learned of the abusive policies that caused the environment to deteriorate, and came to realize that resources don't belong to those who govern but to everyone. Those resources must be protected because if they aren't used in a just manner, they will always be under threat.

Due to the activist dimension of their work, Wangari and the Green Belt Movement had to fight not just the clearing of forests, drought and desertification but Kenya's dictatorial government as well.

"Our people have been persuaded to believe that because they are poor, they lack ... knowledge and skills to address their challenges."

Kenya was a British colony from 1920 until 1963, at which time, after a series of rebellions, it gained its independence. Colonization was an expansionist movement of the most powerful — in economic and military terms — European countries that targeted countries on other continents considered to be less developed. The same phenomenon played out repeatedly and, over the course of the nineteenth century, it primarily affected Africa, which was divided up among different European countries, mostly for the extraction of its raw materials. Using the excuse of bringing European civilization to those countries, Europeans indiscriminately plundered their resources, scorned or stamped out their cultures and, often, massacred their people. The impact of European colonialism on Africa is still apparent today and is at the root of many of its current conflicts given the absurd borders that were drawn up separating ethnic groups that had coexisted peacefully prior to colonization, and joining together enemy ethnic groups that still continue to clash. The names of people and places were Europeanized, customs and ways of being were altered, and the relentless destruction of the natural environment began.

Wangari lived through the colonial era, which she criticized roundly, but she also valued a few positive aspects such as education and health. In the religious school, she learned to read and write. For her, learning to write was new since her culture did not use written language: knowledge was passed down through the oral tradition from one generation to the next via legends and tales. But Wangari was aware that any colonized population loses its ancestral knowledge, its identity and its relationship to nature. She was convinced that only a people alive to its cultural roots could live in peace with its surroundings. And so, she advocated tirelessly for the rediscovery of those roots and a respect for trees and nature and the knowledge and values that had been lost under colonization. Only then would survival be possible.

The seizure and inequitable distribution of lands, and the obligation to pay taxes in currency (which they didn't have since their interactions were based on trading livestock) obliged many men (including Wangari's father) to leave their lands and their families and to work on the colonizers' lands. Muta found work as a laborer on a farm where he was on good terms with the landowner. Soon afterward, Wangari and her mother were able to join him. They helped on the farm and the owner granted them some land to produce their own food. If they wanted to sell their products, they could only sell them to the landowner, who bought them at rock-bottom prices. The owner gave them corn flour and a liter of milk every day in payment for their work. Wangari's family lived there until colonialism ended with the declaration of independence in 1963. Since her father was well regarded by the owner, the man returned the lands he had appropriated as a colonizer. Muta, with other farmers, created a cooperative and lived there until the day he died.

"Responsible governance of the environment was impossible without democratic space."

In 1952, the Land and Freedom Army, called Mau Mau by the British, began an armed struggle against colonial rule. The repressive measures adopted by the British government were extreme: entire towns were destroyed and many forests were burned down to prevent the guerrillas from hiding there. Over one hundred thousand Kenyans died over five years. In 1963, independence was finally won and Jomo Kenyatta was appointed prime minister, but instead of a change of course, he continued the colonial legacy of deforestation and resource exploitation. In 1978, he was replaced by Daniel arap Moi, who stuck to the same policy for another twenty-four years, privatizing the forests and becoming a dictator who governed by wielding the weapons of fear and repression.

Moi and his corrupt policies showed Wangari that there would be no peace nor protection of the environment without a democratic government, and that her commitment to the environment needed to be a political commitment as well. Wangari rebelled against the dictatorship. But it wasn't easy because, as an African woman, there were things she could not do — for instance, call into question anything the men did or confront them. At around the same time, she got a divorce from her husband. Along with his problems with alcohol dependency, he refused to admit that a woman could be as or more intelligent and well-informed as a man was. So he tried to confine her to her role as wife and mother. Her separation affected her personally and socially, its litigation led to her financial ruin, and the separation also resulted in the loss of her position at the university. It was a setback, but she would later acknowledge that it allowed her to do what she wanted without restrictions, since a person's limits should not be decided by the social context but by that person's own abilities.

There were three turning points in her political fight. The first took place in 1989 in Uhuru Park, the only public park in Nairobi. With international assistance, the government had decided to build a sixty-floor-plus skyscraper and a four-floor-high statue of the president there. Through the Green Belt Movement, Wangari wrote a letter of protest to the British government, criticizing its plan to fund a building in Nairobi that it would never have accepted in Hyde Park. Hearing this, Moi was furious and insulted her publicly, wondering how a simple woman dared rebel against a president. It wasn't an easy time for Wangari, but the international community withdrew its funding and the park continued to serve as the city's green lungs. Above all, citizens realized that if one woman could achieve what she had achieved, then they too could do the same: it was in their hands, it was possible!

The second turning point occurred in 1992. A group of women, led by Wangari, met in the Freedom Corner of Uhuru Park to call for the release of their sons and family members who had been imprisoned for political reasons. The women had made up their minds not to leave until their demands were met. Others kept joining them until the government began repressive measures. Although Wangari and many other women were brutally beaten, they did not give up and returned the next day. The battle went on for an entire year until the dictator finally released the prisoners (some of whom, however, were later murdered). What Wangari had accomplished (always within legal means and putting her own life at risk given that she was under constant police surveillance) was to demonstrate civil society's ability to effect the change it wanted to see.

The third turning point took place in 1998, in the Karura forest not far from Nairobi when the government ordered its deforestation. Wangari and the Green Belt

Movement showed up to plant trees, defying government workers. There was a huge public mobilization. Everyone wanted to save the forest. After a year's worth of protests and repression, the government withdrew from the forest and the trees were spared.

Eventually, the mobilizations, which attracted increasingly massive turnouts, toppled the government of dictator Moi who finally called for elections in 2002. Wangari was elected in her district with almost one hundred percent of the vote. In the reformist government that was formed, she was appointed assistant minister for the environment, not minister, and was obliged to fight with the minister in place to be allowed to act, drafting new forest legislation, for instance, which the government ended up defeating.

After beatings at the hands of the army over years of peaceful struggle on behalf of the environment and democratic government, Wangari now urged the army to plant trees outside their barracks and asked them, symbolically, to carry their weapon in their left hand and a seedling in the right. It was in this context, when the wounds of repression and the roots of both the forests and the culture were beginning to heal, that Wangari Maathai was awarded the Nobel Peace Prize. This was a prize which, added to the fifty-some others she was awarded over her lifetime, encouraged her to keep fighting in Kenya and worldwide until her death on September 25, 2011. There could be no letting down of the guard: the struggle continued and continues still today!

"We are called to assist the Earth to heal her wounds and in the process heal our own."

Looking after your home so it doesn't collapse around you, even if it is done out of selfishness, is the right thing to do. But that is not all Wangari tells us. She invites us to go a step further, to "embrace the whole creation in all its diversity, beauty and wonder." And that will be possible if we stop navel-gazing and seeing ourselves as the center of the world. We must instead understand that we are part of the world, co-responsible and co-creators, secure in the knowledge that we belong to one great family and that, insofar as something is done to one family member, however insignificant it may seem, whether it be a tree or an insect on the other side of the world, it is done to us as well.

This is what Wangari tells us in her 2004 speech after thirty years of fighting for sustainable development, democracy and peace, and after having planted more than thirty million trees in Kenya. And this is what we are experiencing today as the climate emergency waits for no one. It is up to us to meet its challenges, knowing that we are going through a shift in consciousness during which, as Wangari said, we must banish fear and give hope to each other. However utopian the challenge may seem, many people have laid down their lives for it.

Wangari's speech is convincing because her words are founded on the moral high ground of her actions and on her ability to inspire others, persuading them that we must leave the world a better place than we found it.

She addresses this message to young people in particular so they will pursue a dream, not of riches but of human progress: a dream to further the budding awareness that will make possible a new way of relating to the Earth, to all her creatures and to ourselves.

Not that we are obliged to accomplish great things: sometimes it is enough to begin by planting a tree or ferrying a drop of water. Wangari often told a story that originated from the Quechua people of South America about a hummingbird. The story takes many forms, including the one below:

> One day there is a huge fire in the forest. All the forest animals flee and are transfixed as they watch the fire burning from afar. All except the little hummingbird who, with its tiny wings, flies back and forth to the stream to throw onto the flames a few drops of water it carries in its beak. After a while, a hedgehog watching the hummingbird's flights to and fro says, "But, hummingbird, are you crazy? Do you really think you can put out the fire?" And the hummingbird says, "I already know I can't; I'm doing the best I can."

Each and every one of us doing the best we can. And doing so today because the Earth can wait no longer:

> The stream has dried up, women walk long distances for water which is not always clean, and children will never know what they have lost. The challenge is to restore the home of the tadpoles and give back to our children a world of beauty and wonder.

Source Notes

Page 68: *Taking Root: The Vision of Wangari Maathai.* Directed and produced by Lisa Merton and Alan Dater, Marlboro Productions, 2008.

Page 78: Yahgulanaas, Michael Nicoll. *Flight of the Hummingbird: A Parable for the Environment.* Vancouver: Greystone Books, 2008.